DEPRECIATION AND DISPOSALS

Revision Workbook

Teresa Clarke FMAAT

DEPRECIATION AND DISPOSALS

BY TERESA CLARKE FMAAT

WORKBOOK

Introduction

I have written this workbook to assist students who are studying bookkeeping or accountancy. It is not designed as a teaching tool but more of a revision workbook. I hope it will help you to consolidate your studies so that you can become more confident with this subject and enable you to feel more comfortable with those tricky exam questions.

Chapter 1 – Depreciation

Adjustments for depreciation are applied in real life and most businesses will apply adjustments for this at the end of their accounting year to create accurate accounting records.

The accruals concept is a principle of accounting which requires the recording of expenses when they are incurred and depreciation is an example of this. The value of non–current assets reduces each year, mainly due to wear and tear, and this reduction is known as depreciation.

We record the estimate of depreciation in the accounting records as a depreciation expense in the statement of profit and loss. We record the lower value of the asset in the statement of financial position by deducting the accumulated depreciation from the cost of the asset and this is known as the carrying value.

The DEAD CLIC rules can be applied to the recording of depreciation and I will be referring to this. Here is a reminder of this rule.

Debits increase:

Expenses

Assets

Drawings

Credits increase:

Liabilities

Income

Capital

We will be looking at the three more common methods of calculating depreciation which are the ones which you will need to be able to apply in your studies.

These are:

The <u>straight-line method,</u>

The <u>diminishing balance</u> or <u>reducing balance method</u> and,

The <u>units of production</u> method.

Chapter 2 – THE STRAIGHT-LINE METHOD

This method depreciates the non-current asset over a given useful life. The formula to calculate this is:

Cost of the asset – estimated residual value
Expected useful life in years

Let's look at an example.

A piece of machinery is purchased for £3,000. It has an estimated useful life of 5 years. At the end of this time, it will have a scrap value of £500.

Cost of the asset (£3,000) – estimated residual value (£500)
Expected useful life in years (5 years)

And to simply that:

£3,000 – £500
5 years

£2,500
5 years

So, £2,500 divided by 5 years = £500 per year

The depreciation expense for each year is £500.

In an exam question, this is sometimes given as a percentage. For example, you may be told that 'depreciation is applied using the straight-line method at 20% on cost with no residual value'.

In this case you will start with the cost of the non-current asset and apply the percentage to this.

Let's look at an example:

A business purchases a machine for £3,000 and depreciates this at 20% straight line with no residual value.

(Cost of the asset - residual value) x 20%.

£3,000 - £0 (as there is no residual value in this example) x 20%

£3,000 x 20% = £600.

The depreciation expense for each year is £600.

Remember:
When calculating depreciation using the straight-line method, you must take the cost, <u>deduct the residual value,</u> and then divide by the years of expected useful life.

CHAPTER 3 – THE DIMINISHING BALANCE METHOD OR REDUCING BALANCE METHOD

For this method, a fixed percentage (which will always be given to you in an exam question) is deducted from the cost of the item, and then the same percentage is deducted from the reduced balance for the second year.

Let's look at an example:

A delivery van is purchased for £10,000 and depreciates this using the diminishing balance method at percentage of 15%. (Note that I will be rounding my answers to the nearest pound and exam questions will usually ask you to do the same. Always read the question).

Year 1 – £10,000 x 15% = £1,500
Year 2 – (£10,000 – £1,500) x 15%
        £8,500 x 15% = £1,275
Year 3 – (£8,500 – £1,275) x 15%
        £7,225 x 15% = £1,084
Year 4 – (£7,225 – £1,084) x 15%
        £6,141 x 15% = £921

The balance or carrying value each year is used to calculate the depreciation. The depreciation expense amount reduces each year as does the balance, hence the diminishing or reducing balance method. I have put these answers into the table below so you can see then clearly.

Year	Balance (£)	Depreciation (£)
1	10,000	1,500
2	8,500	1,275
3	7,225	1,084
4	6,141	921

Using a table like this to calculate depreciation in an exam question makes it much easier to see and means that you are less likely to make mistakes.

An exam question may ask you to calculate the depreciation for a certain year, say year 3, so by drawing up a table like this, you can work out the depreciation and clearly identify the answer required for the task.

CHAPTER 4 – THE UNITS OF PRODUCTION METHOD

This method is usually the most difficult for students to master, so I will try to explain this using some simple figures first.

Depreciation is calculated using the number of units a machine can produce or the number of hours it will be able to be in use. Then it is calculated by the number of units made or the actual number of hours it will work for.

Let's look at a couple of examples:

A piece of machinery is purchased for £300,000 and is expected to produce 100,000 units in its life, after which it will be disposed of with no residual value.

Let's take a look at the first 2 years depreciation charges:

In year 1, we expect to produce 20,000 units.
In year 2, we expect to produce 30,000 units.

Year 1
Cost of the asset x (units for the year/total units)
£300,000 x (20,000/100,000)
£300,000 x 0.2 = £60,000

The depreciation expense for Year 1 is £60,000.

Note: This can also be expressed as a percentage:

£300,000 x ((20,000/100,000) x 100))

£300,000 x 20% = £60,000

Choose whichever method makes sense to you and stick to it.

Year 2

Cost of the asset x (units for the year/total units)

£300,000 x (30,000/100,000)

£300,000 x 0.3 (or 30%) = £90,000

The depreciation expense for Year 2 is £90,000.

If the task provides total hours of use for a machine and the hours per year, you would be exactly the same method, but substituting the word 'units' for 'hours'. Don't let the format of the question confuse you.

CHAPTER 5 – JOURNAL ENTRIES FOR DEPRECIATION

The journal entries for depreciation are straight forward but can be confusing.

The depreciation charge for the year is an expense associated with that year, so this is the <u>depreciation charge expense</u>. Because this is an expense it is a debit in the depreciation charge expense ledger and is transferred to the Statement of Profit and Loss at the end of the year. The credit entry for this transaction is <u>accumulated depreciation</u>. This is always *attached* to the asset cost account which both get carried over to the Statement of Financial Position.

Remember: Use the word expense when you are referring to the depreciation charge and you will see that this is the debit entry according to DEAD CLIC, i.e., an increase in an expense account is a debit.

If we put this into practice, we can look back at the previous example where the depreciation charge for Year 1 was £60,000. The depreciation charge is the expense for the year and its opposite entry goes to the accumulated depreciation.

We can put that into the appropriate ledgers or T accounts:

Depreciation Charge Expense

Debit	£	Credit	£
Accumulated Depreciation	60,000		

Note that the narrative in the depreciation charge expense ledger is the opposite account, the accumulated depreciation.

Accumulated Depreciation

Debit	£	Credit	£
		Depreciation Charge	60,000

Note that the narrative in the accumulated depreciation ledger is the opposite account, the depreciation charge expenses.

The accounts are balanced off at the end of the first year like this:

Depreciation Charge Expense

Debit	£	Credit	£
Accumulated Depreciation	60,000	Statement of P & L	60,000
	60,000		60,000

Note that depreciation charge expense ledger is transferred to the Statement of Profit and Loss at the end of the year as this is an expense.

Accumulated Depreciation

Debit	£	Credit	£
Balance c/d	60,000	Depreciation Charge	60,000
	60,000		60,000
		Balance b/d	60,000

Note that the accumulated is carried down to the next period and this remains in the Statement of Financial Position alongside the original cost account until such time as the asset is disposed of. We will look at disposals later.

For Year 2 the entries will be similar:

Depreciation Charge Expense

Debit	£	Credit	£
Accumulated Depreciation	90,000	Statement of P & L	90,000
	90,000		90,000

Note that depreciation charge expense ledger is transferred to the Statement of Profit and Loss at the end of the year as this is an expense.

Accumulated Depreciation

Debit	£	Credit	£
Balance c/d	150,000	Balance b/d	60,000
		Depreciation charge	90,000
	150,000		150,000
		Balance b/d	150,000

The accumulated depreciation has an opening balance for Year 1, then the charge for Year 2 is added. The balance is then carried down into the next year and remains in the Statement of Financial Position until the asset is disposed of.

When recording the entries in journal style questions they will look like this:

Journal	Debit	Credit
Depreciation charges	£90,000	
Accumulated Depreciation		£90,000

Or more simply:

Dr Depreciation Charges £90,000
Cr Accumulated Depreciation £90,000

Make sure that you are familiar with all three styles as an exam question could ask for any of these formats.

CHAPTER 6 – DISPOSALS

When a non-current asset is sold or disposed of, it is necessary to make adjustments to the accounts. We need to remove the asset and its accumulated depreciation from the ledgers, we need to account for any money received from the sale and we need to calculate the profit or loss on the sale of the asset. We may also need to account for a part-exchange of the asset for a new one.

The disposals account is used to bring all this together and to 'calculate' the profit or loss on the disposal of the non-current asset.

Many students struggle with this task in an exam, so I will take this step by step. Please take your time to understand each point before moving on. You may also find it helpful to note down the steps.

Example:

Kevin disposed of a van which he has originally purchased for £25,000. The sale price was £12,000. The accumulated depreciation at the point of sale was £15,000.

Step 1:
Look at what Kevin had on the day before the disposal and draw up those T accounts or ledgers. He had a van with a cost of £25,000 and accumulated depreciation of £15,000.

Non-current asset – Van

Debit	£	Credit	£
Balance b/d	25,000		

Accumulated Depreciation

Debit	£	Credit	£
		Balance b/d	15,000

Step 2:

On the day of the disposal, we 'remove' the asset and its accumulated depreciation from the ledgers and put them into the disposals account. Each of these is a double entry, so the asset account is credited and the disposal account is debited. Then the accumulated depreciation account is debited and the disposal account is credited. See the ledger accounts below.

Remember: The disposal account is a temporary account that we use to calculate the profit or loss on a sale and the balance is always transferred to the Statement of Profit or Loss.

Non-current asset - Van

Debit	£	Credit	£
Balance b/d	25,000	Disposals	25,000
	25,000		25,000

Accumulated Depreciation

Debit	£	Credit	£
Disposals	15,000	Balance b/d	15,000
	15,000		15,000

Disposals

Debit	£	Credit	£
Non-current asset – van	25,000	Accumulated depreciation	15,000

When balance, both the asset ledger and the accumulated depreciation ledger are empty, and the entries are in the Disposals account.

Step 3: The final adjustment to make to the disposal account before calculating the profit or loss on the sale, is the money received for the sale, the sale price of the van, £12,000.

The money was received by Kevin when he sold the van and he put this into the bank.

DEAD CLIC helps here when we remember that the bank account is an asset and an increase in the asset is a debit. The money goes into the Bank account as a debit and so the Disposals entry is a credit.

Bank

Debit	£	Credit	£
Disposals	**12,000**		

Disposals

Debit	£	Credit	£
Non-current asset – van	25,000	Accumulated depreciation	15,000
		Bank	**12,000**

Note: An exam question will not usually ask you to complete more than one or two accounts, but it is good practice to draw them all to avoid errors.

Step 4: Now that you have three entries in the Disposals account. The only thing left to do is balance this off to work out the profit or loss on disposal.

Disposals

Debit	£	Credit	£
Non-current asset – van	25,000	Accumulated depreciation	15,000
Statement of P & L	**2,000**	Bank	12,000
	27,000		27,000

The balancing figure of £2,000 represents a profit on the disposal of this van. This is transferred to the Statement of Profit and Loss.

The journal entry for the transfer of this is:

Dr   Disposals   £2,000
(because that is what we have done in the ledger)

Cr   Statement of P & L   £2,000
(this shows it is a profit because it is credit, i.e., a form of income according to DEAD CLIC)

Let's just recap on those steps again:

Step 1 – Draw up what you have on the day before the disposal, i.e., the asset and its accumulated depreciation.

Step 2 - Transfer the balances from the asset and accumulated depreciation accounts to the disposals account.

Step 3 – Enter the amount received for the sale into the bank and disposals account.

Step 4 – Balance the account and transfer the profit or loss to the Statement of Profit and Loss.

In that example Kevin sold the van for cash. However, in the next example Kevin part-exchanges his old van for a new one. The steps for this are very similar to the ones for a sale for cash. It is only in Step 3 that we see a difference.

Kevin disposed of a van which he has originally purchased for £25,000. He part-exchanged the van with a part-exchange allowance of £12,000. The accumulated depreciation at the point of sale was £15,000.

Step 1:

Look at what Kevin had on the day before the disposal and draw up those T accounts or ledgers. He had a van with a cost of £25,000 and accumulated depreciation of £15,000.

Non-current asset – Van

Debit	£	Credit	£
Balance b/d	25,000		

Accumulated Depreciation

Debit	£	Credit	£
		Balance b/d	15,000

Step 2:

On the day of the disposal, we 'remove' the asset and its accumulated depreciation from the ledgers and put them into the disposals account. Each of these is a double entry, so the asset account is credited and the disposal account is debited. Then the accumulated depreciation account is debited and the disposal account is credited. See the ledger accounts below.

Remember: The disposal account is a temporary account that we use to calculate the profit or loss on a sale and the balance is always transferred to the Statement of Profit or Loss.

Non-current asset – Van

Debit	£	Credit	£
Balance b/d	25,000	**Disposals**	**25,000**
	25,000		25,000

Accumulated Depreciation

Debit	£	Credit	£
Disposals	15,000	Balance b/d	15,000

Disposals

Debit	£	Credit	£
Non-current asset – van	**25,000**	**Accumulated depreciation**	**15,000**

When balanced, both the asset ledger and the accumulated depreciation ledger are empty, and the entries are in the Disposals account.

Step 3: The final adjustment to make to the disposal account before calculating the profit or loss on the sale, is the part-exchange value of £12,000.

No money was received by Kevin in this case. Instead, the £12,000 was made as part payment for the new van. As this was part payment for the new van, the debit entry is in the new van ledger account.

Non-current asset – new van

Debit	£	Credit	£
Disposals	**12,000**		

Disposals

Debit	£	Credit	£
Non-current asset – van	25,000	Accumulated depreciation	15,000
		Non-current asset – new van	**12,000**

Note: The entry is in exactly the same place as the bank entry for a cash sale, but the narrative is the new van account instead of bank.

Step 4: Now that you have three entries in the Disposals account, the only thing left to do is balance this off to work out the profit or loss on disposal.

Disposals

Debit	£	Credit	£
Non-current asset – van	25,000	Accumulated depreciation	15,000
Statement of P & L	**2,000**	Non-current asset – new van	12,000
	27,000		27,000

The balancing figure of £2,000 represents a profit on the disposal of this van. This is transferred to the Statement of Profit and Loss.

Now you can see that there is no reason to fear those part-exchange style questions. We will look at these in more detail in the following tasks.

Chapter 7 – Tasks with worked answers

Task 1:

You are working on the accounts for Mavis and her year-end is 31 December 2021. Mavis disposed of a hydraulic hoist for £18,000 cash on 18 February 2021. The hydraulic hoist had originally cost £55,000 when Mavis purchased the asset in March 2018. Depreciation was applied at 20% diminishing balance. Depreciation is applied in the year of acquisition but none in the year of disposal.

1. Calculate the total depreciation for the hydraulic hoist.
2. Calculate the profit or loss on disposal by completing the disposals account.

1.

26940

2.

Disposals

Debit	£	Credit	£

Task 1: Worked answer:

You are working on the accounts for Mavis and her year-end is 31 December 2021. Mavis disposed of a hydraulic hoist for £18,000 cash on 18 February 2021. The hydraulic hoist had originally cost £55,000 when Mavis purchased the asset in March 2018. Depreciation was applied at 20% diminishing balance. Depreciation is applied in the year of acquisition but none in the year of disposal.

From the information I have underlined, we can calculate the accumulation depreciation.

Workings:
The year-end for the accounts is 31st December and we can identify that the hydraulic hoist was originally purchased in March 2018. We can calculate the depreciation in the year of acquisition and then each year after, but nothing in the year of disposal.

Year 1: January 2018 – December 2018
£55,000 (cost) x 20% = £11,000

Year 2: January 2019 – December 2019
(£55,000 - £11,000) x 20%
£44,000 x 20% = £8,800

Year 3: January 2020 – December 2020
(£44,000 - £8,800) x 20%
£35,200 x 20% = £7,040

Year 4: January 2021 – December 2021
This is the year of disposal, so no depreciation is applied.

Total accumulated depreciation is the total of the above:

Year 1 £11,000
Year 2 £8,800
Year 3 £7,040

Total = £26,840

1. Calculate the total depreciation for the hydraulic hoist.
2. Calculate the profit or loss on disposal by completing the disposals account.

1.

£26,840

2.

Step 1: Draw up the T accounts for the asset and accumulated depreciation on the day before the disposal. Note: Even though these are not needed for the task, it is good practice to draw them to ensure the task is completed correctly.

Asset – Hydraulic Hoist

Debit	£	Credit	£
Balance b/d	**55,000**		

Accumulated Depreciation

Debit	£	Credit	£
		Balance b/d (as calculated above)	26,840

Step 2: Transfer those balances into the disposals account.

Asset – Hydraulic Hoist

Debit	£	Credit	£
Balance b/d	55,000	Disposals	55,000
	55,000		55,000

Accumulated Depreciation

Debit	£	Credit	£
Disposals	26,840	Balance b/d (as calculated)	26,840
	26,840		26,840

Disposals

Debit	£	Credit	£
Asset – Hydraulic hoist	55,000	Accumulated depreciation	26,840

Step 3:   Enter the cash received for the sale into the bank and the disposals account.

Remember: When money is paid into the bank this is increasing the asset and according to DEAD CLIC assets are increased as debits. Another way to remember this is *money Drives into the bank and Crashes out.*

Bank

Debit	£	Credit	£
Disposals	18,000		

Disposals

Debit	£	Credit	£
Asset – Hydraulic hoist	55,000	Accumulated depreciation	26,840
		Bank	18,000

Step 4: Balance the disposals account to show the transfer to the Statement of Profit or Loss.

Disposals

Debit	£	Credit	£
Asset – Hydraulic hoist	**55,000**	**Accumulated depreciation**	**26,840**
		Bank	**18,000**
		Transfer to P & L	**10,160**
	55,000		**55,000**

In this task you will see that the balancing figure of £10,160 is transferred to the Statement of Profit and Loss on the credit side. This represents a loss on the sale of the asset.

This can be shown as a journal entry as:

Dr	**Statement of Profit or Loss**	**£10,160**
Cr	**Disposals**	**£10,160**

Task 2:

You are working on Ollie's accounts for the year ended 31 March 2021. Ollie sold a machine for £22,000 cash on 20 December 2020. He had originally purchased the machine for £80,000 on 10 June 2016. Depreciation was calculated at 20% straight line assuming no residual value. Depreciation is charged on the year of acquisition but none in the year of disposal.

1. Calculate the total accumulated depreciation for the machine.
2. Calculate the profit or loss on the sale by completion of the disposals account.

Note the accounting year end date of 31 March in your calculation of the accumulated depreciation.

1.

2.

2016	1	16.000	
2017	2	16000	64000
2018	3	16000	
2019	4	16000	
2020	5	—	
2021		—	

Disposals

Debit	£	Credit	£
P+L	6000		

MACHINE
80000

ACCUM
64000 | 64000

DISP.
80000 | 64000   Bank
6000 | 22000

84000 | 16000

Task 2: worked answer

You are working on Ollie's accounts for the year ended 31 March 2021. Ollie sold a machine for £22,000 cash on 20 December 2020. He had originally purchased the machine for £80,000 on 10 June 2016. Depreciation was calculated at 20% straight line assuming no residual value. Depreciation is charged on the year of acquisition but none in the year of disposal.

1. Calculate the total accumulated depreciation for the machine.
2. Calculate the profit or loss on the sale by completion of the disposals account.

Note the accounting year end date of 31 March in your calculation of the accumulated depreciation.

Workings for the accumulated depreciation:
(Cost − residual value) x 20% straight line = yearly depreciation charge
(£80,000 − 0) x 20% = £16,000

The yearly depreciation charge is £16,000.

How many years?

The accounting year is 1 April to 31 March, so

Year 1 (the year of acquisition) 1 April 2016 to 31 March 2017 − £16,000
Year 2   1 April 2017 to 31 March 2018 - £16,000
Year 3   1 April 2018 − 31 March 2019 - £16,000

Year 4   1 April 2019 – 31 March 2020 - £16,000

Year 5   (the year of disposal) 1 April 2020 – 31 March 2021   £0

It is always a good idea to write out the years to avoid mistakes in counting how many years of depreciation are needed.

Total depreciation is therefore 4 years at £16,000 = £64,000

1.

£64,000

2.

Step 1: Draw up the T accounts for the asset and accumulated depreciation on the day before the disposal. Remember that it is good practice to draw all the T accounts to avoid errors.

Asset – Machine

Debit	£	Credit	£
Balance b/d	80,000		

Accumulated Depreciation

Debit	£	Credit	£
		Balance b/d (as calculated)	**64,000**

Step 2: Transfer those balances into the disposals account.

Asset – Machine

Debit	£	Credit	£
Balance b/d	**80,000**	**Disposals**	**80,000**
	80,000		**80,000**

Accumulated Depreciation

Debit	£	Credit	£
Disposals	**64,000**	**Balance b/d**	**64,000**
	64,000		**64,000**

Disposals

Debit	£	Credit	£
Asset – Machine	80,000	Accumulated depreciation	64,000

Step 3: Enter the cash received for the sale into the bank and the disposals account.

Bank

Debit	£	Credit	£
Disposals	22,000		

Disposals

Debit	£	Credit	£
Asset – machine	80,000	Accumulated depreciation	64,000
		Bank	22,000

Step 4: **Balance the disposals account to show the transfer to the Statement of Profit or Loss.**

Disposals

Debit	£	Credit	£
Asset – machine	8,0000	Accumulated depreciation	64,000
Transfer to P & L	6,000	Bank	22,000
	86,000		86,000

In this task you will see that the balancing figure of £6,000 is transferred to the Statement of Profit and Loss on the debit side. This represents a profit on the sale of the asset.

This can be shown as a journal entry as:

Dr	Disposals	£6,000
Cr	Statement of profit and loss	£6,000

Task 3:

Mary buys a new tractor for £65,000. She pays for this with £40,000 from the bank and £25,000 part-exchange allowance from her old tractor. The old tractor was purchased some years ago for £55,000. The accumulated depreciation at the point of the disposal of the old tractor was £28,000.

1. Calculate the profit or loss on disposal by completing the disposals account.

Disposals

Debit	£	Credit	£
Old tractor	55 000	Accumm. dep.	28000
		25 000	25000
		P+ 2000	2000
	55 000		55000

2. Draw up the ledger to account for the purchase of the new tractor.

New tractor

Debit	£	Credit	£
Bank	65000		£
Bank	40,000		
Disposal	25 000		

Accum.
28000 | 28000

Disposal
55000 | 28000
40 | 25000
       2000 lost
55000 | 55000

Bank
40000

Task 3: Worked answer

Mary buys a new tractor for £65,000. She pays for this with £40,000 from the bank and £25,000 part-exchange allowance from her old tractor. The old tractor was purchased some year ago for £55,000. The accumulated depreciation at the point of the disposal of the old tractor was £28,000.

1. Calculate the profit or loss on disposal by completing the disposals account.

In this question we have been given the balances for the old tractor and the accumulated depreciation. Even though this question involves a second part where we need to account for the new tractor, we start it in exactly the same way as the previous tasks.

Step 1: Draw up the asset and accumulated depreciation accounts on the day before the disposal. Here I will put this in journal style format, but you might find it beneficial to keep drawing the T accounts on paper for the time being.

Old tractor
Dr Balance b/d   £55,000

Accumulated depreciation
Cr Balance b/d   £28,000

Step 2: Transfer those balances into the disposals account.

Old tractor
Cr Disposals   £55,000

Accumulated depreciation
Dr Disposals   £28,000

Disposals

Debit	£	Credit	£
Old tractor	**55,000**	**Accumulated depreciation**	**28,000**

Step 3: Enter the amount received for the old tractor, the sale price. Or, in this case, enter the part-exchange allowance.

Disposals

Debit	£	Credit	£
Old tractor	**55,000**	**Accumulated depreciation**	**28,000**
		New tractor	**25,000**

Note: The narrative for the part-exchange is the new asset account rather than the bank. This is because Mary did not receive cash for the sale of the tractor, but instead received an allowance of £25,000 towards the purchase price of the new tractor.

Step 4: Balance the account to work out the profit or loss on the sale.

Disposals

Debit	£	Credit	£
Old tractor	55,000	Accumulated depreciation	28,000
		New tractor	25,000
		Transfer to P & L	2,000
	55,000		55,000

We can see that the balancing amount is on the credit side of the disposals account and this is transferred to the Statement of Profit or Loss as a loss on disposal.

2. Draw up the ledger to account for the purchase of the new tractor.

In the second part of this question, we are asked to complete the ledger account for the new tractor. If you look back at the disposal account above, you will see that the part-exchange allowance was entered as a credit there, so the opposite entry is a debit in the new tractor account. This represents part-payment of the new tractor.

New tractor

Debit	£	Credit	£
Disposals	**25,000**		

We are told in the question that Mary paid £40,000 from her bank account, so we can enter that into the bank ledger and the new tractor account.

Using DEAD CLIC we can remember that the money out of the bank is a credit (as this reduces the asset) and the new tractor account is a credit as the asset value is increasing.

New tractor

Debit	£	Credit	£
Disposals	**25,000**	**Balance c/d**	**65,000**
Bank	**40,000**		
	65,000		**65,000**
Balance b/d	**65,000**		

If we check back to the question, we can see that the total cost of the new tractor was £65,000 and this is now shown in the ledger account above as the balance b/d.

Task 4:

Manda bought a new excavator on 30 April 2020 for a total cost of £360,000. She part-exchanged her old excavator for £100,000 and paid the balance from the bank. The old excavator had originally been purchased on 31 May 2018 for £280,000. She depreciated this at 30% straight line and depreciation is applied on a monthly basis.

1. Calculate the accumulated depreciation on the old machine at the point of disposal.
2. Calculate the profit or loss on the disposal of the old machine by completing the disposals account.
3. Complete the accounting entries for the new excavator, clearly showing the balance b/d.

1.

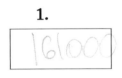

84000

31/May/2018 M m 49000
30/Apr/2020 12 m 84000
          4 m 28000
          ___
          161

2.

Disposals

Debit	£	Credit	£
Old Machine	280000	Accumm	161000
	100000		100000
		Loss	19000

NEW 360000 |

OLD 280.000 | 280000

old 161000 | 161000

Old Disposal
10,000 | 280000
280000 | 161000
100000 |

3.

New excavator

Debit	£	Credit	£
Disposal	100000	Bal b/d	36000
Bank	26000		
	36000		

Note: The accumulated depreciation in this task is calculated on a monthly basis, so you need to calculate the depreciation for the total time the machine was owned.

Note: You have not been given the cost of the new excavator, so you will need to work this out.

old machine   Accum   Disp.

280.000 | 280000   161000 | 161000   280.000 | 161000

P+L 119000

Bank

Task 4: Worked answer

Manda bought a new excavator on 30 April 2020 for a total cost of £360,000. She part-exchanged her old excavator for £100,000 and paid the balance from the bank. The old excavator had originally been purchased on 31 May 2018 for £280,000. She depreciated this at 30% straight line and depreciation is applied on a monthly basis.

1. Calculate the accumulated depreciation on the old machine at the point of disposal.

The old excavator was purchased on 31 May 2018 and disposed of on 30 April 2020, so we need to calculate how many months it was owned. Be careful to count all the full months and don't be afraid to use your fingers!

Whole months –   June 2018 to May 2019 = 12 months
June 2019 to April 2020 = 11 months
Total months of ownership is 23 months.

Depreciation is calculated at 30% straight line, so we need to work out what it is for one year first.

Cost x 30% = yearly depreciation charge
£280,000 x 30% = £84,000

We can now work out the monthly depreciation charge.

£84,000 / 12 months = £7,000

The excavator was owned for 23 months so we multiply the monthly depreciation charge by the months.

£7,000 x 23 months = £161,000 = accumulated depreciation

1.

£161,000

2. Calculate the profit or loss on the disposal of the old machine by completing a disposals account.

We can use the disposals steps again for this question. This is a good point to remember what we will be expecting to see in this account. The disposal account will always look something like this before it is balanced.

Disposals

Debit	£	Credit	£
ASSET	X	ACCUMULATED DEPRECIATION	X
		BANK / NEW ASSET	X

Let's remind ourselves of the steps to arrive at this.

Step 1: Draw up the asset and accumulated depreciation account on the day before the disposal.

Step 2: Transfer those balances into the Disposals account.

Step 3: Add the amount received for the sale or the part–exchange value.

Step 4: Balance the account and transfer the profit or loss to the Statement of Profit and Loss.

Disposals

Debit	£	Credit	£
Old excavator	**280,000**	**Accumulated depreciation**	**161,000**
		New excavator	**100,000**
		Transfer to P & L	**19,000**
	280,000		**280,000**

The balance transferred to the profit and loss represents a loss on the sale of the old excavator.

3. Complete the accounting entries for the new excavator, clearly showing the balance b/d.

We can see the entry in the disposals account above for the part exchange allowance towards the new excavator. We need to complete the double entry into the new excavator account below, clearly showing the part-exchange allowance which represented part-payment of the new excavator.

New excavator

Debit	£	Credit	£
Disposals	**100,000**		

We are told that the balance was paid from the bank, so we need to use a little maths to work this out.

When we refer back to the question, we can see that the total cost of the new excavator was £360,000. The part-exchange allowance given on the old machine was £100,000, so the balance is the amount paid from the bank.

New excavator

Debit	£	Credit	£
Disposals	100,000	Balance c/d	360,000
Bank	260,000		
	360,000		360,000
Balance b/d	360,000		

Note: The balance brought down in the new excavator cost account is £360,000, which represents the total cost of the machine.

Chapter 8 – Tasks (answers at the end of the book)

Task 5:

Ollie purchases a piece of machinery for £37,000. He expects it to have a useful life of 10 years with a residual or scrap value of £7,000. He uses the straight-line method of depreciation.

Calculate the depreciation charges for the first 3 years from this information.

$$\frac{37\ 000 - 7000}{10} = 3000$$

$$3000 \times 3 = 9000$$

Task 6:

Billy purchased a new taxi for £42,000. His depreciation policy is to depreciate vehicles at 15% diminishing balance.

a) Calculate the depreciation charge for years 1, 2 and 3. Round your answers to the nearest whole pound.

a) Calculate the carrying value at the end of year 3.

42000

1   35700   6300

2   30345   5355

3   25793   4552
                 _____
             16207.

|
↓
✓

Carrying value

Task 7:

Reesa purchased a crisp making machine on 30 August 2016 for £800,000. It was estimated to have a useful life of 200,000 hours.

Calculate the depreciation for the following years based on the hours of production method.

Year 1: 2016   10,000 hours

Year 2 2017   80,000 hours

Year 3 2018   70,000 hours

Year 4 2019   30,000 hours

Year 5 2020   10,000 hours

Handwritten working:

$40,000$

$= 800000 \times (40000 / 200000)$

$80000 \times (80,000/200000) = 320000$

280000

120000

40000

Remember: To calculate this depreciation you use the hours of production in each year divided by the total hours and multiply this by the cost of the machine.

Handwritten: Machine / 80000

Task 8:

You are working on the accounts of Anastasia Haulage for the year ending 31 December 2020.

Anastasia sold a lorry on 10 February 2020 for £45,000 cash. The lorry has originally been purchased for £80,000 in April 2017.

Anastasia's depreciation policy for lorries is 20% reducing balance with a full year's depreciation in the year of acquisition and none in the year of disposal.

1. Complete the following table to calculate the accumulated depreciation on the lorry prior to sale.

Year	Depreciation charge	Carrying value
2017	80.000 → 16 000	64000
2018	12 800	51200
2019	10240	40960
2020	—	
Total	39040	40960

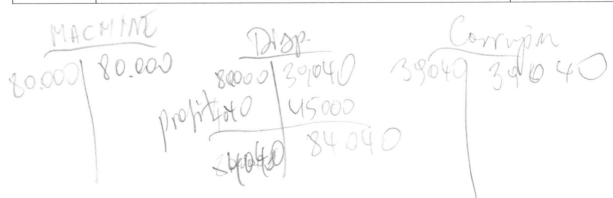

2. Complete the Disposals account clearly showing the transfer to the Statement of Profit and Loss.

Disposals

Debit	£	Credit	£

3. Identify where Anastasia Haulage has made a profit or loss on the sale of this lorry.

PROFIT ON SALE / LOSS ON SALE

Task 9:

Lareck purchased a new delivery van on 1 January 2021 for £32,000. He paid for this with £15,000 from the bank, with the remaining balance being paid with the part-exchange allowance for his old van.

The old van had originally been purchased on 1 September 2018 for £28,000.

Lareck depreciates his vans at 20% straight line based on the number of months of ownership.

1. Calculate the accumulated depreciation on the old van at the point of disposal. Round your answer to the nearest pound.

   Remember: Calculate the depreciation for each year and multiply by the number of months of ownership.

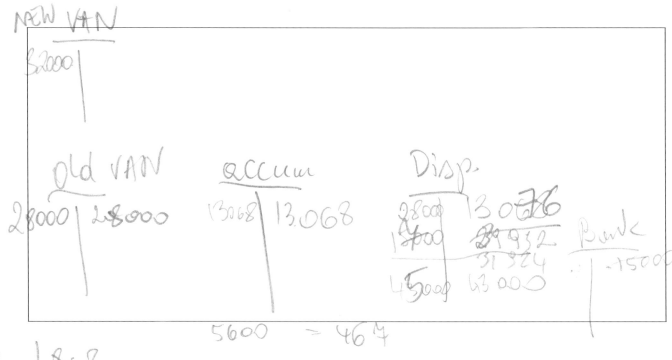

2. Calculate the profit or loss on disposal of the old van.

Note: You have not been given the part-exchange allowance amount so you will need to work this out.

Disposals

Debit	£	Credit	£
Old Van	28000	accumulated	13076
		new VAN	17000
P+L	2076		
	30076		30076

3. Make entries for the purchase of the new delivery van.

New delivery van

Debit	£	Credit	£
Bank	15000		
Disposal	17000		

Task 10:

Alicja purchased a new weaving machine in December 2020. She paid for this with £10,000 cash and a part exchange allowance of £6,000 for her old weaving machine.
The old weaving machine had originally cost her £14,000. 3 years depreciation has been applied at 20% per year straight line.

1. Complete the disposal account below, clearly showing the transfer to the Statement of Profit and Loss.

Disposals

Debit	£	Credit	£
old machine	14000	Acceuleled	8400
P+L	400		600
	14400		14400

2. Identify whether this was a profit or loss in the Statement of Financial Position.

Profit / Loss

3. What was the total cost of the new weaving machine?

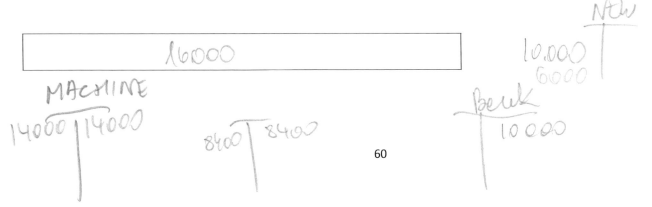

| 16000 |

NEW
10.000
6000

Beuk
10 000

MACHINE
14000 14000

8400 8400

Task 11:

Complete the following sentences:

1. The ...._straigh line_.............. method of depreciation uses a fixed

   percentage and multiplies this by the carrying amount of the asset

   each year.

2. The balance in the disposals account is transferred to the Statement

   of ...._profit and loss_.........

3. The double entry for depreciation is debit ...._dep. expense_............

   and credit ...._accumuleted depreciation_......

4. Depreciation is an accounting adjustment and is therefore a

   cash/non-cash transaction.

5. The diminishing balance method of depreciation is also known as the

   ...._reducing_............. balance method.

Task 12:

You are working on the accounts for Marjorie who has a financial year end of 31 December 2020.

Marjorie purchased a delivery van for her flower selling business on 1 December 2018 for £22,000 cash paid from the bank. She depreciates the van using the straight-line method at 20% with estimated residual value of £2,000.

Complete the ledger entries for the year ended 31 December 2020 to account for the depreciation. Balance off the ledgers as appropriate. **Note: You are only required to make entries for the current year.**

Depreciation charge expense

Debit	£	Credit	£
Accumulated	4000		
		bal c/d	4000
	4000		4000

Accumulated depreciation

Debit	£	Credit	£
		Balance b/d	8,000
c/d	12000	Dep.	4000
	12000		12000

VAN

22000

Task 13:

1. Explain how to calculate depreciation using the straight-line method.

2. Explain how to calculate depreciation using the diminishing balance method.

3. Explain how to calculate depreciation using the units of production method.

4. Give an example of when it would be appropriate to use the straight-line method.

5. Give an example when it would be appropriate to use the diminishing balance method.

6. Give an example of how a business might apply the units of production method.

Task 14:

This question is going to test your understanding.
Remember:
Note the year end you are working on.
Note the depreciation method you are using.
Calculate the years/months correctly.
Use the steps we discussed earlier in the workbook.
Make sure that you balance the accounts correctly.

You are working on the accounts for Joe for the year ending 31 March 2021.

Joe purchased a new computer on 1 December 2020 for £1,200. He was given a £200 part-exchange allowance for his old computer which he had originally purchased on 30 November 2018 for £1,000.

Joe depreciates his computer using 30% straight line method and applies depreciation for every month of ownership.

1. Calculate the accumulated depreciation for the old computer on the day of disposal.

600

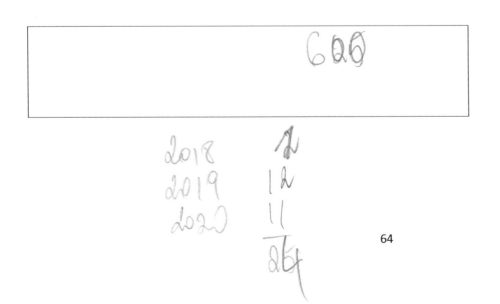

2. Complete the disposals account for the old computer, clearly showing the transfer to the Statement of Profit and Loss.

Disposals

Debit	£	Credit	£
old computer	1000	accumulated	680
		New comp.	200
P+L	200 →		
	1000		1000

3. Complete the entries for the purchase of the new computer.

New computer

Debit	£	Credit	£
Disposal	200		
Bank	1000	c/d	1400
	1400		1400

CHAPTER 9 – ANSWERS

Task 5:

Ollie purchases a piece of machinery for £37,000. He expects it to have a useful life of 10 years with a residual or scrap value of £7,000. He uses the straight-line method of depreciation.

Calculate the depreciation charge for the first 3 years from this information.

Answer:

<u>**Cost – residual value**</u>
Years of useful life

<u>**£37,000 – £7,000**</u>
10 years

<u>**£30,000**</u> = **£3,000 per year**
10 years

Year 1 = £3,000
Year 2 = £3,000
Year 3 = £3,000

Note that using the straight-line method, the amount of depreciation charge per year will be the same.

Task 6:

Billy purchased a new taxi for £42,000. His depreciation policy is to depreciate vehicles at 15% diminishing balance.

a) Calculate the depreciation charge for years 1, 2 and 3. Round your answers to the nearest whole pound.

b) Calculate the carrying value at the end of year 3.

Answer:

a) **Cost x 15%, then carrying value or balance x 15%**

A table format is much easier for this type of answer:

Year	Calculation	Depreciation charge	Carrying value
1	£42,000 x 15%	£6,300	£35,700
2	£35,700 x 15%	£5,355	£30,345
3	£30,345 x 15%	£4,552 (rounded)	£25,793

By completing this table, we have the answer for part b) too. The carrying value is shown in the last cell, £25,793.

It is good practice to draw a table for this type of question to avoid errors.

Task 7:

Reesa purchased a crisp making machine on 30 August 2016 for £800,000. It was estimated to have a useful life of 200,000 hours.

Calculate the depreciation for the following years based on the hours of production method.

Year 1: 2016   10,000 hours
Year 2 2017   80,000 hours
Year 3 2018   70,000 hours
Year 4 2019   30,000 hours
Year 5 2020   10,000 hours

Remember: To calculate this depreciation you use the hours of production per year divided by the total hours and multiply this by the cost of the machine.

Answer:

Cost x (hours of operation/total hours of operation)
£800,000 x (10,000/200,000)
£800,000 x 0.05 = £40,000
OR
£800,000 x 5% = £40,000

So, let's put that into a table and complete the rest of the calculations:

Year 1: 2016   10,000 hours

Year 2 2017   80,000 hours

Year 3 2018   70,000 hours

Year 4 2019   30,000 hours

Year 5 2020   10,000 hours

Year	Hours of operation	Calculation	Depreciation charge
1	10,000	£800,000 x (10,000/200,000)	£40,000
2	80,000	£800,000 x (80,000/200,000)	£320,000
3	70,000	£800,000 x (70,000/200,000)	£280,000
4	30,000	£800,000 x (30,000/200,000)	£120,000
5	10,000	£800,000 x (10,000/200,000)	£40,000

The depreciation charges vary each year depending on the hours of production that the machine is used for.

Remember that the hours used in this task could be substituted for units in another, but the method is the same.

Task 8:

You are working on the accounts of Anastasia Haulage for the year ending 31 December 2020.

Anastasia sold a lorry on 10 February 2020 for £45,000 cash. The lorry has originally been purchased for £80,000 in April 2017.

Anastasia's depreciation policy for lorries is 20% reducing balance with a full year's depreciation in the year of acquisition and none in the year of disposal.

1. Complete the following table to calculate the accumulated depreciation on the lorry prior to sale.

Year	Depreciation charge	Carrying value
2017	£80,000 x 20% = **£16,000**	**£64,000**
2018	£64,000 x 20% = **£12,800**	**£51,200**
2019	£51,200 x 20% = **£10,240**	**£40,960**
2020	Nil as this is the year of disposal	
Total	**Accumulated depreciation = £39,040**	

2. Complete the Disposals account clearly showing the transfer to the Statement of Profit and Loss.

Disposals

Debit	£	Credit	£
Lorry	**80,000**	**Accumulated depreciation**	**39,040**
Transfer to P & L	**4,040**	**Bank**	**45,000**
	84,040		**84,040**

3. Identify where Anastasia Haulage has made a profit or loss on the sale of this lorry.

PROFIT ON SALE / _LOSS ON SALE_

We can check whether this is a profit or a loss by drawing the journal entry for this, i.e., the double entry.

Journal	**Dr**	**Cr**
Disposals	**£4,040**	
Statement of P & L		**£4,040**

You can see that the Statement of Profit or Loss entry is a credit. When we think back to DEAD CLIC, a credit is a form of income, so this is a profit.

Note: If the entry in the Statement of P & L had been a debit and we think back to DEAD CLIC, a debit is a form of expense, so this would be a loss.

Task 9:

Lareck purchased a new delivery van on 1 January 2021 for £32,000. He paid for this with £15,000 from the bank, with the remaining balance being paid with the part-exchange allowance for his old van.

The old van had originally been purchased on 1 September 2018 for £28,000.

Lareck depreciates his vans at 20% straight line based on the number of months of ownership.

1. Calculate the accumulated depreciation on the old van at the point of disposal. Round your answer to the nearest pound.
   Remember: Calculate the depreciation for each year and multiply by the number of months of ownership.

> Cost – residual value x 20% = one year's depreciation charge
> £28,000 – £0 (no residual value given) x 20% = £5,600
> £5,600 / 12 months = £467 per month (rounded)
> Whole months of ownership:
> September 2018 – August 2019 = 12 months
> September 2019 – August 2020 = 12 months
> September 2020 – December 2020 = 4 months
> Total months of ownership = 28 months
> Months of ownership x Monthly depreciation charge
> 28 months x £467 = **£13,076** = **accumulated depreciation**.

2. Calculate the profit or loss on disposal of the old van.

Workings to calculate part-exchange allowance:
New delivery van total cost = £32,000
Payment made from bank = £15,000
Therefore, the part-exchange allowance = £17,000 (32,000 − 15,000)

Disposals

Debit	£	Credit	£
Old delivery van	**28,000**	**Accumulated depreciation**	**13,076**
Transfer to P & L	**2,076**	**New delivery van**	**17,000**
	30,076		**30,076**

3. Make entries for the purchase of the new delivery van.

New delivery van

Debit	£	Credit	£
Disposals	**17,000**	**Balance c/d**	**32,000**
Bank	**15,000**		
	32,000		**32,000**
Balance b/d	**32,000**		

Task 10:

Alicja purchased a new weaving machine in December 2020. She paid for this with £10,000 cash and a part exchange allowance of £6,000 for her old weaving machine.

The old weaving machine had originally cost her £14,000. 3 years depreciation has been applied at 20% per year straight line.

1. Complete the disposal account below, clearly showing the transfer to the Statement of Profit and Loss.

Workings for the depreciation: In this example you are just told that 3 years depreciation has been applied. The original cost was £14,000 and the depreciation method is 20% straight line.

Remember: Don't look for more in the question than is given. This is a straight calculation of £14,000 x 20% and multiplied by 3 years.

Disposals

Debit	£	Credit	£
Old weaving machine	**14,000**	**Accumulated depreciation**	**8,400**
Transfer to P & L	**400**	**New weaving machine**	**6,000**
	14,400		**14,400**

2. Identify whether this was a profit or loss in the Statement of Financial Position.

If you are unsure about this, complete the journal entry:

Dr Disposals £400
Cr Statement of Profit or Loss £400

The entry in the Statement of Profit or Loss is a credit. If we think back to DEAD CLIC, this is a form of income, therefore a profit.

**Profit** / _Loss_

3. What was the total cost of the new weaving machine?

We were told that Alicja paid £10,000 from her bank account and she was given £6,000 part exchange allowance from the old weaving machine. Therefore, the total cost of the new weaving machine is £16,000 (£10,000 plus £6,000).

Task 11:

Complete the following sentences:

1. The ...**DIMINISHING BALANCE**.. method of depreciation uses a fixed percentage and multiplies this by the carrying amount of the asset each year.

2. The balance in the disposals account is transferred to the Statement of ...**PROFIT OR LOSS**....

3. The double entry for depreciation is debit ...**DEPRECIATION CHARGES (DEPRECIATION CHARGE EXPENSES)**.

   and credit ...**ACCUMULATED DEPRECIATION**...

4. Depreciation is an accounting adjustment and is therefore a cash/***NON-CASH*** transaction.

   The diminishing balance method of depreciation is also known as the ...**REDUCING**.. balance method.

Task 12:

You are working on the accounts for Marjorie who has a financial year end of 31 December 2020.

Marjorie purchased a delivery van for her flower selling business on 1 December 2018 for £22,000 cash paid from the bank. She depreciates the van using the straight-line method at 20% with estimated residual value of £2,000.

Complete the ledger entries for the year ended 31 December 2020 to account for the depreciation. Balance off the ledgers as appropriate.
Note: You are only required to make entries for the current year.

Workings for depreciation:
Cost – residual value x 20%
(£22,000 - £2,000) x 20% = £4,000

Depreciation charge expense

Debit	£	Credit	£
Accumulated depreciation	**4,000**	**Transfer to SOPL**	**4,000**
	4,000		**4,000**

You are only required to make entries for the current year. You will see that there is a balance brought down from the previous year in the accumulated depreciation and you are required to add this year's charge to it before balancing the account with a balance c/d.

Accumulated depreciation

Debit	£	Credit	£
Balance c/d	**12,000**	**Balance b/d**	**8,000**
		Depreciation expense	**4,000**
	12,000		**12,000**
		Balance b/d	**12,000**

Task 13:

1. Explain how to calculate depreciation using the straight-line method.

Suggested answer: (note that your answer does not have to match this answer, but may give you some tips on how to explain it).

To calculate depreciation using the straight-line method, you need to take the original cost of the non-current asset, deduct the estimated residual or scrap value, if any, and then divide this by the number of expected years of life. Alternatively, you may multiply the figure by a given percentage. This can be expressed like this:

<u>Cost – residual value</u>
Years of useful life

Or
(Cost – residual value) x percentage given

2. Explain how to calculate depreciation using the diminishing balance method.

Suggested answer:
To calculate depreciation using the diminishing balance method, you first multiply the cost of the non-current asset by the percentage given. For the next year you take the carrying amount of the non-current asset (which is the cost less the accumulated depreciation) and multiply this by the same percentage. You will see that each year the depreciation charge gets lower and the carrying value gets lower too.

This can be shown like this:

Year 1 – Cost x percentage = depreciation charge

Year 2 – Carrying value x percentage = depreciation charge

3. Explain how to calculate depreciation using the units of production method.

Suggested answer:

To calculate depreciation using the using of production method, you first need to know the number of units the non-current asset can produce in its lifetime and the cost of the non-current asset. Then you find out how many units are to be used (or have been used) each year and calculate the units for the year as a percentage of the total units and multiply the original cost by this.

It can be shown like this:

Total units of production of the non-current asset in its lifetime = 100,000

Cost of non-current asset = £200,000

Year 1 – 25,000 units are produced.

(25,000 units / 100,000 units) x cost

0.25 x £200,000 = depreciation charge

0.25 x £200,000 = £50,000

4. Give an example of when it would be appropriate to use the straight-line method.

Suggested answer:

The straight-line method is more commonly used where an item has a known lifetime and is used constantly over that time.

For example, a chocolate flavoured crisp machine purchased for £250,000 for a contract lasting just 5 years with a scrap value of £50,000 and used consistently over the 5 years would have the same amount of depreciation for each year of its useful life.

This would be shown like this:

(£250,000 - £50,000) / 5 years = £40,000 depreciation per year

5. Give an example when it would be appropriate to use the diminishing balance method.

Suggested answer:

The diminishing balance is more commonly used when an item does not have a definitive life and loses more value in the earlier years than in the later years. A good example for this method would be a delivery van because this does not have a specific useful life and could certainly be in use for many years if looked after. Also, it loses more value in the early years than in the later years.

6. Give an example of how a business might apply the units of production method.

Suggested answer:

This method is used so that the depreciation is charged according to the wear and tear on the machine. It is only applied when the machine is used. If a machine is used for just a few units then less depreciation is charged.

This can be shown like this:

Total units of production of the non-current asset in its lifetime = 100,000

Cost of non-current asset = £200,000

Year 1 – 25,000 units are produced.

(25,000 units / 100,000 units) x cost

0.25 x £200,000 = depreciation charge

0.25 x £200,000 = £50,000

Task 14:

This question is going to test your understanding.
   Remember:
Note the year end you are working on.
Note the depreciation method you are using.
Calculate the years/months correctly.
Use the steps we discussed earlier in the workbook.
Make sure that you balance the accounts correctly.

You are working on the accounts for Joe for the year ending 31 March 2021.

Joe purchased a new computer on 1 December 2020 for £1,200. He was given a £200 part-exchange allowance for his old computer which he had originally purchased on 30 November 2018 for £1,000.

Joe depreciates his computer using 30% straight line method and applies depreciation for every month of ownership.

1. Calculate the accumulated depreciation for the old computer on the day of disposal.

Two things to think about here – the months to apply and the actual calculation of depreciation.

Months:

Purchase date 30 November 2018

Disposal date 1 December 2020

Remember to calculate whole months, so:

1 December 2018 – 30 November 2019 = 12 months

1 December 2019 – 30 November 2020 = 12 months

Total 24 months

Depreciation:

Cost – residual value x 30%

£1,000 - £0 (none in the question) x 30%

£1,000 x 30% = £300 per year

£300 is for 12 months and we want 24 months of depreciation.

£300/12 = depreciation for one month, then multiply by 24

(or use your own method, so long as you get the right answer)

£600 accumulated depreciation

2. Complete the disposals account for the old computer, clearly
   showing the transfer to the Statement of Profit and Loss.

Disposals

Debit	£	Credit	£
Old computer	**1,000**	**Accumulated depreciation**	**600**
		New computer	**200**
		Transfer to SOPL	**200**
	1,000		**1,000**

**Note: The entry is on the credit side of the disposals account, so will be
a debit in the Statement of Profit or Loss. Debits accordingly to DEAD
CLIC are expenses so this represents a loss on disposal.**

3. Complete the entries for the purchase of the new computer.

Note: The question did not give the amount paid from the bank, so you need to work this out from the information given. You are told that the new computer cost £1,200 and the part-exchange allowance was £200, so the balance for the purchase of the new computer is the difference of £1,000. £1,200 – £200 = £1,000.

New computer

Debit	£	Credit	£
Disposals	**200**	**Balance c/d**	**1,200**
Bank	**1,000**		
	1,200		**1,200**
Balance b/d	**1,200**		

When balanced this is carried down into the next year because this is an asset and still owned. The amount carried down is the total cost of the new computer.

I hope you have found this workbook useful. If you have any comments you can find me on my Facebook page: Teresa Clarke AAT Tutoring.

Teresa Clarke FMAAT

Printed in Great Britain
by Amazon

74570552R00052